Just Chill

Navigating Social Norms and Expectations

ABDO
Publishing Company

A GUY'S GUIDE

Just Chill

Navigating Social Norms and Expectations

by MK Ehrman

Content Consultant
Dr. Robyn J. A. Silverman
Child/Teen Development Expert and Success Coach
Powerful Words Character Development

Credits

Published by ABDO Publishing Company, 8000 West 78th Street, Edina, Minnesota 55439. Copyright © 2011 by Abdo Consulting Group, Inc. International copyrights reserved in all countries. No part of this book may be reproduced in any form without written permission from the publisher. The Essential Library™ is a trademark and logo of ABDO Publishing Company.

Printed in the United States of America,
North Mankato, Minnesota
062010
092010

 THIS BOOK CONTAINS AT LEAST 10% RECYCLED MATERIALS.

Editor: Amy Van Zee
Copy Editor: Richard Reece
Interior Design and Production: Marie Tupy
Cover Design: Marie Tupy

Library of Congress Cataloging-in-Publication Data
Ehrman, MK
 Just chill : navigating social norms and expectations / MK Ehrman ; content consultant, Robyn J. A. Silverman
    p. cm. — (Essential health : a guy's guide)
Includes index.
ISBN 978-1-61613-542-3
1. Young men—Conduct of life. 2. Young men—Life skills guides. 3. Communication. I. Silverman, Robyn J. A. II. Title.
BJ1671.E37 2011
646.700835'1—dc22
                                    2010017055

contents

Dr. Robyn Silverman truly enjoys spending time with young people. In fact, it's what she does best! As a child and teen development specialist, Dr. Robyn has devoted her career to helping guys just like you become all they can be—and possibly more than they ever imagined. Throughout this series, you'll read her expert advice on friends, girls, classmates, school, family, and everything in between.

A self-esteem and body image expert, Dr. Robyn takes a positive approach to life. She knows how tough it is to be a kid in today's world, and she's prepared with encouragement and guidance to help you become your very best and realize your goals.

Dr. Robyn helps young people share their wildest dreams and biggest problems. Her compassion, openness, and honesty make her trusted by many adolescents, and she considers it a gift to be able to interact with the young people whom she sees as the leaders of tomorrow. She created the Powerful Words Character Development system, a program taught all over the world in martial arts and other sports programs to help guys just like you become examples to others in their communities.

As a speaker, success coach, and award-winning author, Dr. Robyn's powerful messages have reached thousands of people. Her expert advice has been featured in *Prevention* magazine, *Parenting* magazine, *U.S. News and World Report*, and the *Washington Post*. She was an expert for *The Tyra Show, Fox News,* and NBC's *LXtv.* She has an online presence, too. You can follow her on Twitter, become a fan on Facebook, and read her blog on her Web site, www.DrRobynSilverman.com. When she isn't working, Dr. Robyn enjoys spending time with her family in New Jersey.

Dr. Robyn believes that young people are assets to be developed, not problems to be fixed. As she puts it, "Guys are so much more than the way the media paints them. They have so many things to offer. I'm ready to highlight how guys get it right and tips for the ways they can make their teen years the best years so far . . . I'd be grateful if you'd come along for the ride."

When I look back at my life, I often say that the hardest job I ever had was growing up. Do you feel like you are at the point in your life where you're no longer a child but not completely an adult? Well, that part was the hardest of all. Time and time again, I used to ask myself, *What do people want from me?* and *What if I screw up?* You might feel that you're alone in wondering if you can live up to peoples' expectations. You might wonder why you even have to. I know I did.

Maybe you're a little confused about how you should act, what you should look like, and what you should say in different situations. Maybe you wonder about things such as money and what to do with it. Perhaps you feel pressure from friends or television to spend your money on certain things so you can look a certain way. What does it mean to be a "real man"? How *are* you supposed to act? What do you do when you are given more freedom to make your own decisions, but more responsibility, too? In this book, you'll read stories about guys who worried about how they looked, how they dressed, and how they talked (particularly to girls!). And there are some guys in this book who deal with the pressure to do some really dangerous things, such as drinking, drugs—or worse. You'll see them make good decisions and some not-so-good decisions.

Not every problem you face is going to have a simple solution. And at one point or another, chances are you're going to make a bad choice about how to act. But with a little effort, willingness to admit your mistakes, and some help from a few important people (such as your friends, your family, and people you look up to) you'll find that you have what it takes to make it through. You'll come out of it better, smarter, and more mature than when you started. That's what it means to "grow up."

In the meantime, don't forget to have fun. While you may face problems and confusion, you're also entering one of the best times of your life. You can do more things, see more places, and get to know more people. And when things don't quite work out the way you hoped, it doesn't mean something is wrong with you. Instead, these situations are an opportunity to make yourself even better. So step up to the plate and see what happens.

Good luck,

MK

1
The Full-Court Press

With money comes something we didn't really expect: responsibility. That is, the responsibility to make wise decisions about what to do with it. Should you save it? Spend it? And if so, on what?

It's hard enough to think clearly about what to do with your money. But it's even harder when you are the target of advertising that constantly tries to make you spend it on tons of different products. Did you know that your age group is one of the groups that advertisers focus on the most? And what do you do when everybody suddenly shows up listening to the same music

player or wearing the same label? Sometimes that's enough to make you feel like a freak or a loser or to make you wonder if maybe everybody knows something you don't. That's kind of what happened to Luther. You could say he knows what it's like to experience a "full-court press."

Luther's Story

Ever since he was old enough to walk, Luther's life revolved around basketball. After dinner, he'd run out to shoot a few hoops in the driveway before it got too

Did you know that your age group is one of the groups that advertisers focus on the most? And what do you do when everybody suddenly shows up listening to the same music player or wearing the same label?

dark. On weekend afternoons, he'd head down to the park where there was always a pickup game. Luther was tall, a fast dribbler, and a good shooter. He never had to worry about being picked last for a team.

When Luther got to junior high, he easily made the starting team. But when he showed up to the first practice, he noticed something. His teammates were all wearing basketball shoes with familiar logos. Luther, on the other hand, was wearing some plain athletic shoes his mom had picked up from some discount department store. For the first time he could remember, Luther felt embarrassed and unsure of himself on a basketball court.

Think About It

- Have you ever had an experience like Luther's? What happened?
- Is it important for Luther to wear the same kind of shoes as everyone else? Why or why not?

Luther made an announcement at dinner that night: "Mom, Dad, I need new sneakers."

"What's wrong with the ones you have?" his mother asked. "They're almost new."

"They're just not right!" Luther finally said, looking down at the table.

"Well," said his dad, "if you want new sneakers, you can pay for them with the money you made mowing lawns this summer."

"But Dad, you know I'm saving that to buy NBA tickets!" Luther exclaimed.

"Sorry, Son," his father told him. "But that's how it is. We can't afford to buy you everything you may want."

Think About It

- What did Luther mean when he said that his sneakers were "not right"? Was that a good answer to his mom's question? Why or why not?

- Have you ever had a situation where you wanted two things but only had money for one? What was it? What did you do?

At school, Luther ran into his coach and decided to talk with him about the situation.

"Coach Braden," he asked, "do I need to get myself some different sneakers?"

The coach looked puzzled. "The rules say only that you need to show up in uniform and wear acceptable athletic footwear. Is there any reason why you think the ones you have are not acceptable?"

Luther explained that everyone seemed to be wearing the same brand that the NBA players wore—the kind advertised on billboards and at the mall. Luther, on the other hand, wore a brand nobody had ever heard of.

"Well, Luther," Coach Braden said, "it's true that some of those brands have features that might be helpful with your game: extra cushioning, more flexibility, and things like that. On the other hand, you might be paying extra just for a name and a design. It's up to you whether you want to pay extra for those things. All I care about is that you play the best game you possibly can, and the same goes for your teammates." The coach gave Luther some magazines with reviews of new athletic shoes by people who didn't work for the shoe companies. "Maybe these can help you decide," he said.

Think About It

- Does the fact that a professional player recommends a certain brand of shoe mean that the brand is somehow better? Why or why not? Have you ever bought something just because a celebrity recommended it?

- Why do you think the coach gave Luther those magazines? Couldn't he have just told him what to do and which shoes to buy? Why didn't he?

At the mall, Luther went into an athletic shoe store and started trying on shoes. Next to the shoes, there were life-size cardboard cutouts of the NBA stars who recommended them. He tried on the pair with the same design and logo that most of his new teammates wore. "How much are they?" he asked the salesperson. "Those just came out," the salesperson replied. "They're $180." That was all the money Luther had. As he reached into his gym bag, the coach's magazines accidentally spilled out. He realized that he hadn't even read them yet, and the NBA tickets weren't sold out yet. Besides, no one was going to kick him off the team today for wearing his old shoes.

"Can I ring them up for you?" the salesperson asked. Luther looked at his feet with the new shoes. His plain shoes were on the floor next to them.

"Thanks," he finally answered, "but I have some research to do first."

Think About It

- What do you think Luther eventually decided to do? What would you have done? Why?

- What do you think went through Luther's mind as he looked at the new basketball shoes and his plain shoes?

Luther learned that for every choice, there's a sacrifice. Making his choice even more difficult is the advertising everywhere he looks: on television, on the streets, at sports events, even in video games! And a lot of it is directed right at Luther and other guys his age. The ads often show the kinds of people young guys might want to be. They try to make people associate those qualities they admire with the product or the brand and its very identifiable logo. When more people buy into the brand, it becomes harder for the rest not to join the pack. A situation like this becomes more than just a question of money. It is also a question of our ability to think clearly in the face of a great deal of pressure.

Talking about decisions with someone you trust can often help you make wiser choices. And of course, the more you can educate yourself, the better. Then you're on your way to growing into not only a smart consumer but also a secure and self-reliant adult.

Work It Out

1. Make a list of your wants and needs. Get a good idea of things you really need, those you really want, and what you probably can do without.

2. Seek advice. Ask other people who own the product about their experiences. Get input from people who know about the product. Search independent reviews on the Internet and in your library. Remember, advertisements exist to get you to buy!

3. Take your time. An impatient purchase is often a regretted one.

4. Become media literate. Learn to sift through the information you receive. Understand that images, words, and colors are carefully chosen to get you to buy.

The Last Word from MK

Today, we grow up in a world full of logos, brands, and ads, ads, ads. When you reach the point where you have to start making decisions about what to do with your own money, you begin to realize that sacrifices have to be made. If you buy one thing, you can't afford something else. Resist pressure. Whether it's from guys your age, a salesperson, or advertising on television, don't let yourself feel pressure to buy something before you decide that it's what you want or need.

2 Financial Freedom

Few people forget their first job. There's something satisfying about earning money for work you've done. It makes you feel like you're on your way to being an independent adult. Making your own money might give you the chance to spend it on some extra things. Sometimes, though, it can make you forget how much you still rely on your parents for most of your needs. Making your own money does allow you some extra freedom, but your parents will probably still insist on some limits.

What should these limits be? Well, that's up to each family to work out. And "work out" can sometimes mean getting into conflict. This might sound like a

bad thing, but it doesn't have to be. As Sam is about to learn, getting into conflict with your parents isn't the end of the world. As a matter of fact, learning to handle conflict sensibly is actually an important step on the road to adulthood.

Sam's Story

At 6:00 p.m., Sam brought the last of the dogs, Lucy, a big mixed breed, back to the Greenwalds' house and was done for the day. About two months ago, his parents told him they would provide Sam with everything he needed, but if he

Making your own money does allow you some extra freedom, but your parents will probably still insist on some limits.

wanted to buy any "luxuries," he would have to pay for them himself. And that meant getting a job. It was their way of teaching him how to be responsible with money.

Sam came up with the idea of walking his neighbors' dogs, and it had worked out really well. He walked six dogs a day, twice a day, for a dollar a dog. Sam carefully put away half his earnings, and his savings added up quickly. His parents kept his savings for him, marking down how much money he'd earned on a board on the refrigerator. Today, he was ready to spend it.

"Mom, Dad," he said when he got home, "can I have my money now? There's something I want to get."

"Sure," his Dad answered. "The money's yours. What are you going to get?"

"A dog," Sam answered.

When his father said, "No way!" Sam was angry and disappointed.

Think About It

- Have you ever saved up for something and found out later that your parents wouldn't let you buy it? What was it? What happened?

- Do you think Sam deserved to get a dog if he saved up the money for it? Why or why not?

"But Dad!" Sam protested. "You said the money was mine."

"Yes, it's yours," his Dad responded. "But you're still my son, and your mother and I make the rules in this house. And we say no to getting a dog."

Sam got very angry. "That's not fair!" he said. "You lied to me!"

"That's no way to talk to your parents," his dad replied. "This is still our house, and while you're here, you live by our rules."

Within a day or two, people started calling Sam's house, wondering why he didn't come by to walk their dogs. Sam didn't even answer the phone. He just let it go to voice mail. When his mom discovered all the messages, she wanted to know why Sam stopped working.

"Why should I make money if I can't even spend it on what I want?" he asked.

His mom thought for a second and said, "I think it's time we called a family meeting."

Think About It

- what do you think of Sam's dad's reasons for not allowing him to get a dog?

- what do you think about Sam's decision not to work anymore? How would you have handled the situation?

When Sam's dad got home, they all sat around the kitchen table. Sam pointed out the reason he got a job in the first place was because they said he needed to learn how to manage his own money. Now that he wanted to make a decision, they wouldn't let him.

His dad explained to Sam that getting a dog was not like getting a new shirt. Even though Sam had a lot of experience walking dogs, taking care of one full-time was a big responsibility—one that would affect the entire family.

"Have you researched anything about training a dog?" he asked. "Do you know how much work it is to train a puppy? They need a lot of care and attention."

Sam admitted that he hadn't. "If I learn all about it, then can I get one?" he asked.

"Well," his mom said, "why don't you do some research. Think about it for a while. If you still want a dog by your sixteenth birthday, we can consider it then. That way, we know you're not rushing into a bad decision. Is that a deal?"

It sounded reasonable to Sam. "Okay," he said, grabbing his jacket and heading out the door.

"Where are you going?" his father asked him.

"I gotta get over to the Greenwalds' right away," he said. "Otherwise, I'm going to lose a customer."

Think About It

- what do you think about the solution that Sam's family worked out? Would you be satisfied with it if you were Sam? Why or why not?

- Why did Sam suddenly start to care about losing customers when he hadn't cared before?

Conflict often arises when a guy's desire to be independent clashes with his parents' desire to maintain control and set boundaries for acceptable behavior. In this case, Sam was trying to demonstrate his independence by getting a dog. He had worked for the money, after all. Shouldn't he be allowed to spend it as he sees fit? His parents, on the other hand, are concerned that Sam might be making a serious mistake. And they are still the ones who make the rules in the house.

There are no easy answers here. But we can still point to a few factors that helped the issue of the dog to come to a successful resolution—at least for now. Notice that when Sam and his family speak angrily to one another, nothing is accomplished. Through calm and open communication, however, Sam is able to better understand why his parents behaved the way they did. Sam's parents, in turn, can get a better idea of where Sam is coming from. It is only then that they are able to work out a solution—one that recognizes that parents still have authority, but one that also allows Sam to demonstrate enough maturity and responsibility to make a decision about getting a dog. It's a win-win situation.

Work It Out

1. Conflict, particularly with parents, is a fact of life. Learn to accept these disagreements for what they are. They are not signs that your parents don't love you or don't care about how you feel. The key to maintaining a good relationship in the face of conflict is learning to compromise.

2. You don't resolve conflict by keeping everything to yourself. Learn to tell your parents how you feel, and don't forget the other half of communication: listening.

3. It's okay to say how you feel, but it's a good idea to wait until you're calm to say it. Words spoken out of hurt or anger probably won't help the situation.

The Last Word from MK

Making decisions when you're angry is dangerous. Luckily, instead of taking a step backward, the family was able to work out a solution that helped Sam move toward greater independence and better decision making. Remember how much can be accomplished through honest conversation and learning to compromise.

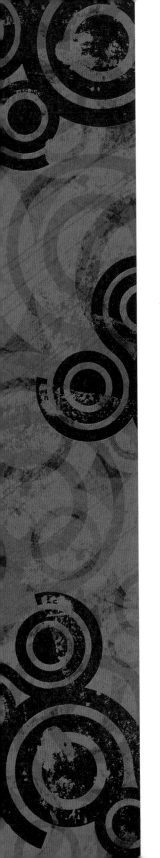

3

Mr. Moneybags

Okay, so who wants money? Easy question, right? Everybody does. Having money allows you to buy the things you want—from a pizza after school to a hot new video game. Just having money in your pocket somehow makes you feel good. But money can be like fire. If you don't handle it wisely, you can get burned.

You'll probably find that the first time you're in charge of spending your own money—like when you get your first real allowance—it creates as many problems as it solves. Do you spend it for something you want now, or save it up for something bigger? And then there's the annoying fact that no matter how

much money you have, you can never buy everything you want.

Trickiest of all is the way having—or not having—money can change the way we look at ourselves and the way others look at us. You know that expression, "Money can't buy you love"? Well, as Manny is about to find out, it doesn't even buy you friendship. Not for long, anyway.

Manny's Story

Manny kept looking at his wallet to make sure he wasn't dreaming, but there it was: a crisp $50 bill. He had never felt richer than he did at that very moment. His parents had decided he was old enough to receive a monthly allowance and today was

You'll probably find that the first time you're in charge of spending your own money—like when you get your first real allowance—it creates as many problems as it solves.

payday! Manny couldn't wait to get to school so he could brag about it, especially to his friend Salim.

During recess, Manny casually took out his wallet and started playing with the bill. It had a big picture of President Ulysses S. Grant and actually changed colors when he tilted it. Other kids gathered around to look. "Manny, where'd you get that?" they asked.

"My parents," he answered smugly. "But it's mine now."

"What are you gonna spend it on?" Salim asked.

"My friends, of course," he answered.

And suddenly, Manny found that he had a lot of friends.

After school, Manny announced he was going out for pizza. "Who wants to come?" Half the class followed him. At the pizza parlor, Manny bought the double jumbo pizza special. Within minutes, it was all gone.

Think About It

- Was it a good idea for Manny to show off his money in front of everyone? Why or why not?

- Have you ever bought things for people just to be popular? What happened?

Afterward, the group passed a video game store. Someone pointed out that a new car racing game was on sale.

"C'mon, Manny, get the game so we can all play it," said Manny's classmate Nate.

"Manny, what are you doing?" Salim whispered to him. "You always said Nate was mean. He and his friends used to ignore you. Why are you buying all that stuff for them?"

But Nate pushed his way in between them and threw his arm around Manny. "So you 'da man' or not, Mr. Moneybags?"

Manny still had plenty of cash left in his wallet, so he figured, *Why not?*

"Okay, video games at my house," he announced. Everybody cheered, and Manny felt better than he had in a long time. He liked being "Mr. Moneybags." He didn't even notice that Salim didn't come along.

Think About It

- why does Salim try to talk Manny out of buying the video game?

- If Nate and his friends were mean to Manny, why does he want to treat them to pizza and a video game?

- Have you ever found yourself trying to do nice things for people who acted like they didn't like you? How did it work out?

Manny's mom soon noticed he was hanging out with a new crowd.

"Where did all these people come from?" she asked him. "And how come I don't see Salim around? I thought he was your friend."

"Salim doesn't like to have fun like these guys do," Manny answered.

"Well, just make sure you're not buying your friends," his mom warned him. "Because at this rate, you won't be able to afford them. You still have three weeks to go before you get your next allowance, so I hope you're putting some money away."

To Manny, the idea of "buying" friends sounded like a joke. "Don't worry, Mom," he said. "I still got plenty left."

Think About It

- What do you think of Manny's mom's advice?

- Do you think people act differently when they have money? In what way?

- Do you think people act differently toward people who don't have money? In what way?

The next week, the kids all followed Manny to the pizza parlor after school. He sat down at the table and was ready to order, but when he looked in his wallet, there was nothing there. He didn't even have any money to buy a small slice for himself!

"Er, sorry guys," he said, a little embarrassed. "I guess I'm out of cash. Maybe somebody else can buy the pizza today."

"What, no pizza money, Moneybags?" Nate said. "In that case, we're outta here." And suddenly Manny was sitting all alone.

"What happened to all your friends, Manny?" he heard someone say. Manny looked up to see Salim was standing by the door.

"You were right about Nate and those guys," Manny said. "I can't believe what an idiot I've been. I'm really hungry now, and nobody would even buy me a small slice."

"Well, at least you know it now," Salim said. "C'mon, let's eat. My treat."

Think About It

- why do you think Manny ran out of money so fast? what should he have done to prevent that?

- Do you get an allowance or make money at a job? Do you have a budget? If no, why not?

- Do you think Manny learned something about money and friendship? If so, what?

"What, no pizza money, Moneybags?" Nate said. "In that case, we're outta here." And suddenly Manny was sitting all alone.

An allowance can be our first true experience with handling money. We might start with some small amount when we're really young—just for a few extras, such as a snack after school—and then as we get older, we become responsible for more and more of the things we buy. This way, we learn about handling money through actual experience. And experience can sometimes be a tough teacher.

Manny made a few basic mistakes. He didn't plan ahead to make sure his money would last him until his next allowance payday. But he also learned something valuable: Money doesn't buy you friendship, and it doesn't make you feel better about yourself. Those things have to be earned in a different way. Now that he's figured that out, he can start the next month a little wiser. He can concentrate on budgeting. And now he knows not to waste his money on things—and people—that can't really be bought anyway.

Work It Out

1. It's not enough just to know how much money you spent and how much you have left. Work out a budget—how much you can afford to spend each day. Once you do that,

you can start spending—and saving—your money wisely.

2. Don't depend on your memory to keep track of your money. Write down where and how you spend your money and make sure your plan adds up!

3. When you think about buying something, always ask whether it's something you actually need or just something you want. It's okay to get things you want; just make sure that the needs come first!

4. Whether you save a lot or a little is up to you. But it's always a good idea to put something away for a "rainy day." A good rule of thumb is 10 percent. You never know when it's going to come in handy.

The Last Word from MK

Manny will probably have a hard time until he gets his next allowance, but that's how it goes with money. The only way you really learn how to handle it is by actually having some, even if you do blow it all on things that really weren't worth it. Making mistakes is just part of the way we learn. The next time around, we can be a little more careful and plan ahead. The most important thing to remember is that some things—like your friends and the way you feel about who you are—don't come with a price tag.

4
The Ladies Man

rowing up, guys and girls are like two sides of an accordion. When you're really young, you all pretty much hang out together. Then as you get a little older, you kind of separate—boys with boys, girls with girls. Then guys start to get interested in girls again in a different and much more confusing way.

Meanwhile, we become very aware of being guys and start to feel like we're supposed to "act like men." The hard part is that we really don't know what that means. In fact, nobody really knows what that means, but that doesn't stop most guys from pretending like they do. While we might get some signals from the television shows we watch or the music we listen to, we're mostly going to look at the other guys we hang around with and act like them. And usually that means acting tough. Sometimes, a guy might even start to disrespect a girl to prove he doesn't like her. But that's not what makes a real man, as Trey will slowly learn.

Trey's Story

It was just another afternoon, and Trey was doing what he usually did: hanging out with his pals, Baxter and Chen. Sometimes they would go to someone's house to play video games, or if the weather was nice, they'd hang out in the park and play Frisbee or basketball. They liked to listen to music, too. Trey was from the South, so he had grown up listening to country music. He even played the guitar. But Baxter and Chen's favorite songs were full of negative words about girls. "Only wimps like that romantic stuff," Baxter would say. Trey didn't want to look weak. So he started listening to the same kind of music.

We become very aware of being guys and start to feel like we're supposed to "act like men." The hard part is that we really don't know what that means.

Trey remembered when he was younger, the boys and girls all basically mixed together, but not anymore. And Baxter and the guys were very antigirl. Mostly, the guys would just order the girls around, as if it were the girls' job to do whatever the guys

wanted. When the girls refused, Chen and Baxter would call them names, the kind of names they'd hear in those songs. Soon, Trey started using those words, too. The girls usually just turned and walked away mumbling things like, "Those boys are so immature," or "Grow up!"

Think About It

- Does the kind of music you listen to say anything about you? What do you think your music taste says?

- Why do you think the boys started being "antigirl"? Have you ever been "antigirl"?

- Have you ever started using a word just because your friends were using it?

One day, Trey was assigned to write a report about how electricity works. He didn't have the slightest idea where to find the answers. He asked Baxter and Chen for help, but they didn't know either. The only person who would know was the smartest kid in their science class, Leticia. Trey and Leticia had been friends when they were younger, but lately they never spoke to each other. Trey tried to approach her, but she just ignored him.

"You have to help," Trey said. "Otherwise, I'm going to fail."

Leticia laughed. "Well, maybe if you don't treat us girls like dirt, some of us might even care," she said and walked away. Trey got angry and started yelling names at her. Leticia didn't even turn around.

Think About It

- Do you think it was right for Leticia not to help Trey? How do you think she felt about the way Trey and his friends talked about girls?

- Have you ever made someone angry with you because of how you spoke about the group he or she belonged to? What happened?

Trey was mad when he got home. He walked through the door and threw his books on the floor.

"What's gotten into you?" his dad demanded. Trey angrily explained what had happened and how Leticia wouldn't help him.

"Well, if you spoke to her the same way you are speaking to me now, no wonder she won't help you," his dad said. "What you're saying sounds a lot like what I hear coming out of your iPod. If you want Leticia's help, you have to treat her with respect."

"What do you mean?" Trey asked.

Trey's dad explained that Trey was probably just beginning to notice how different boys are from girls.

"Sometimes that can feel uncomfortable," his dad said, "but boys will always need girls, and girls will need boys. You all have to learn to get along together."

Think About It

- What do you think of Trey's dad's advice? Has anyone ever given you good advice about how to treat girls? Who was it? What did he or she say?

- What do you think it means to treat girls with respect?

At school the next day, Trey went over to Leticia and apologized. "Hey, Lateesh, I just wanted to let you know that the way I acted to you was wrong.

I don't expect you to help me with my paper, but I still wanted to tell you I was sorry."

"I'm glad you said that," she responded. She was quiet for a minute. Then she said, "You know, my mom can't pick me up today, and I need someone to help me carry all my lab stuff home. Well, maybe if you do that, I'll see what I can tell you about electricity."

Trey used to help Leticia carry things home many times. He hadn't minded it at all, and it was actually kind of fun hanging out with her.

"Deal!" Trey said.

After school, Trey ran into Baxter and Chen. They invited him to go with them to the park, but Trey said no. "Aw, man," Baxter said, "you going to go hang out with that—"

Trey stopped him right there. "She's my friend," he said.

Leticia smiled as Trey came over to help her with some bags. He thought about the school dance that was coming up. Maybe he could even ask her to go.

After school, Trey ran into Baxter and Chen. They invited him to go with them to the park, but Trey said no.

Think About It

- Did apologizing to Leticia make Trey look weak? Did interrupting Baxter before he called Leticia a bad name make Trey look weak? Why or why not?

- Did Baxter and Chen have the right to be angry when Trey didn't hang out with them? Why or why not?

- Do you think Trey and Leticia's relationship will be the same as it was when they were younger, or different? If different, how so?

As you grow up, finding your identity as a man becomes both important and confusing. This is especially true when it comes to relating to girls. Often, we look to television, movies, popular music, and even guys our own age for help in how to act. In these places, you can find both good and bad examples. Just because you see the behavior in action doesn't mean it's right!

It's important to pay attention to what kind of messages you're receiving. Think about the lyrics and language you hear. What are they telling you? In Trey's case, both the music he listened to and his friends offered bad examples, which made it difficult for him to relate again to his old friend Leticia.

Luckily, he was able to find a good example in his dad, who gave him some solid advice about being a man. In the end, Trey was able to learn that you don't make yourself more of a man by disrespecting girls. We are all human—men, women, boys, and girls. And when Trey learns to take responsibility for his actions (by admitting he was wrong and apologizing) and treat Leticia with kindness (by giving her the respect every person deserves), he is well on his way to truly understanding what it means to be a man.

Work It Out

1. Be yourself. There is no reason to act a certain way just because that's how other guys behave (either around you, on television, or in music).

2. Respect others to get respect. Nobody deserves to be treated worse because they're a boy or a girl, black or white, or rich or poor. Learn to respect everyone as a person, and you'll find that you'll also get respect in return.

3. Find positive role models. Look to men you respect (such as your dad, an older brother, or a teacher, for instance) to help you understand the situations that men face today. You'll probably realize you're less alone than you thought.

4. Never try to pick yourself up by putting others down. This shows insecurity, not strength.

The Last Word from MK

Nobody said it was easy to figure out what it means to be a man and how to deal with the opposite sex. But that doesn't mean you need to put extra pressure on yourself by thinking you have to act a certain way. Just remember: you'll never succeed in raising yourself up if it means putting somebody else down.

5

The Brown Bagger

It's going to happen sooner or later, so you'd better get ready. At some point, you'll face the pressure to drink alcohol. We see so much on television and elsewhere that shows drinking as being fun, happy, and cool. It's really hard to understand how dangerous it can be to drink alcohol, especially when you're young.

Alcohol has negative effects on many things, including schoolwork, sports, or even the ability to follow a movie or a conversation. Then there's the damage it does to your body and brain, particularly when you're still developing. And worst of all, like cigarettes, it's very addictive.

The thing is, no kid puts down a soft drink and picks up the hard stuff because he likes the taste. It's usually because there's something missing in a person's life, or he thinks he has something to prove. And focusing on that can help you resist the pressure that says, "If you don't drink, you're not really cool." It's not easy, but it's important. It was an important lesson for Carlos—and one for you, too.

Carlos's Story

Carlos lived alone with his mom. She was a successful businesswoman, so Carlos always had nice clothes and plenty of cool gadgets. The only problem was that his mom moved a lot because of business, so Carlos always had a hard time making friends. And because she was always so involved with work, either going off to meetings or making deals on the phone, Carlos hardly spent any time with her. He was often bored.

It's really hard to understand how dangerous it can be to drink alcohol, especially when you're young.

Carlos was jealous of Justin, a guy at school who always seemed to have friends hanging around him. Carlos often wondered what he needed to do to become part of his group. One day, Carlos was walking home and saw Justin and some other kids going into Justin's house.

"Hey, it's that Carlos kid," Justin called out. "My folks are away so we're going to party. Are you in?" Carlos didn't know what Justin meant, but he didn't want to blow it by sounding like an idiot.

"Sure," he answered, and followed the guys into the house.

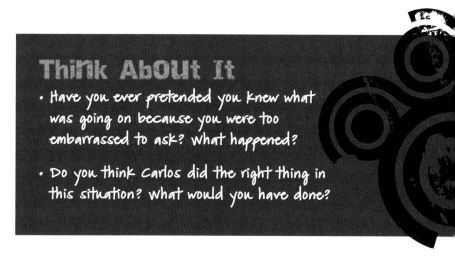

Think About It

- Have you ever pretended you knew what was going on because you were too embarrassed to ask? What happened?

- Do you think Carlos did the right thing in this situation? What would you have done?

In the kitchen, Justin tossed Carlos a can of beer like it was some totally normal thing. Carlos had never before tasted any kind of alcohol.

"You're not still a baby, are you?" Justin asked as Carlos hesitated. Everyone chanted, "Drink! Drink!" until Carlos cracked open the can and drank.

The beer tasted awful. It was foamy and bitter, but Carlos made himself swallow it. When everyone shouted "Yeah!" he took another sip. And then another. The other guys were cracking open cans for themselves, and someone passed him another beer. He drank that, too.

Things got blurrier after that. Carlos barely remembered walking home. His mom wasn't home when he got there. Carlos felt sick that night and thought he was going to throw up the next morning. But his mom didn't mention anything the next day. Carlos got a text that afternoon from Justin. He felt like he'd broken into the group—even if his head was pounding.

Think About It

- If Carlos didn't like the taste of beer, why do you think he kept drinking? What would you have done?

- Have you ever felt pressure to drink alcohol or do something you knew you shouldn't do? What was that like? What did you end up doing?

- Do you think that drinking alcohol is a sign that you're grown up?

A few weeks later, Carlos was called in to see Mr. Ikeda, the guidance counselor.

"Carlos, your teachers have noticed that your grades are dropping and that you don't seem interested in school," he began. "I'm wondering whether something has changed recently? Are you having any problems at home?"

"My mom's been having trouble at work, and she's been needing me to help out extra around the house," Carlos answered, surprised at how easy it was to lie. He didn't have any chores. His mother hired people to do that.

"Well, next week is parent-teacher night," Mr. Ikeda said. "Maybe we can all talk about how to arrange things so your schoolwork doesn't suffer."

But Carlos wasn't worried. His mom was always too busy to attend those things, anyway.

Think About It

- why do you think Carlos started doing poorly at school? Is there one reason, or more than one?

- Do you think Carlos should have told Mr. Ikeda the truth? Have you ever lied to cover up something you didn't want people to know you were doing? What happened?

Carlos liked the idea of having drinking buddies. It sounded very grown up. Justin had an older brother who would sometimes give them a bottle of something. Or, they would try to get people to go into the store and buy alcohol for them. They switched to whiskey because the bottles were smaller and easier to hide. Soon, Justin began bringing bottles to school and secretly "brown bagging," as they called it, in the schoolyard.

"I better get to homeroom," Justin said, holding his almost-empty bottle. "Who wants to finish this?" They had already had a lot to drink, but Carlos liked to show he was braver than anyone else. As he tipped his head back and drank, the schoolyard spun around him. He felt like he was going to be sick. Mr. Ikeda happened to be walking by just then. He had barely asked, "What's going on?" before Carlos doubled over. The bottle fell from his hand and smashed on the ground.

Think About It

- what do you think made Carlos want to prove he was braver than his friends?

- Have you ever done something you shouldn't have done just to feel like you were grown up? What was it?

Twenty minutes later, Carlos was sitting in the nurse's office. He felt like the room was spinning. Mr. Ikeda was there, too, and they were all waiting for Carlos's mother to arrive.

"We were wondering why his grades were falling," Mr. Ikeda said when she finally got there. "Did you know your son was drinking? Have you talked to him about it?"

"I've been so wrapped up in my work," his mother replied. "I had no idea Carlos was drinking." Carlos could tell she was angry.

When they got into the car, Carlos's mom looked at him and said, "I haven't been paying enough attention to you or to what you've been doing. I think you and I need to start talking to each other."

Carlos agreed, but at that moment, he felt too sick to say so.

Think About It

- what do you think will happen to Carlos? will he drink again?

- what effect do you think it will have if Carlos and his mother spend more time together talking? Do you think that will make him less likely to start drinking again? why or why not?

Drinking alcohol is never completely risk-free, even for adults. But for preteens it's downright dangerous. Younger people who drink are more likely to fail in school, to become addicted to alcohol, and to get in trouble with the police. They put their mental, physical, and social health at risk for many other unpleasant consequences as well.

The problem is that as we get older, the pressure to drink becomes more intense. At the same time, we also become more curious about the world around us. On the positive side, because we are more mature, we can understand the facts about alcohol and what it can do. This will help us find the strength to say no, and if necessary, to leave the group when there is pressure to get drunk.

And remember, you don't have to do this alone. Many parents might not be aware of how much of a problem drinking can be at your age, so it might be up to you to tell them if you want their help. You can also talk to a guidance counselor or another adult you trust. He or she can offer valuable suggestions and point you to other resources at school, in the library, or online.

Work It Out

1. Never drink something unless you know what it is. If someone offers you something at a party, ask what it is and where he got it. If you don't like his answer or he doesn't have an answer, don't drink it.

2. Learn to say no. Don't make excuses if you're offered alcohol. This makes it easier for people to talk you into it. Look them in the eye and say, "No, thanks."

3. Avoid friends and situations where you know you'll feel pressure to drink. Friends who pressure you are not true friends.

4. When all else fails, leave. Always have a phone number where you can reach your parents or another responsible adult if you need to be picked up.

5. Remember that there are plenty of fun things to do that don't involve drinking.

The Last Word from MK

So are you getting the message that alcohol is not some fun thing that makes you have friends and feel grown up? The temptation to try alcohol is strong, because advertisements, movies, and television show drinking as being a cool thing to do. But you can be stronger than that. You don't need alcohol to have fun or fit in!

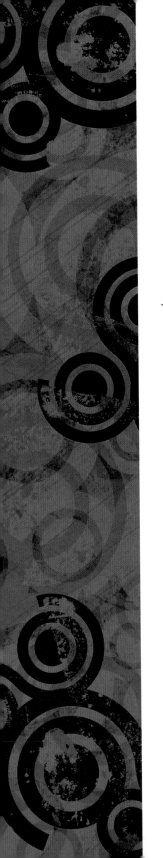

6

The Choker

As you grow up, you start to become aware of all the things life has to offer. It's only natural to be curious and want to experiment. After all, that's a big part of how we learn about ourselves and learn about the world. In most cases, even if we make mistakes, we can pick ourselves up and move on, better and wiser for our experience.

In a few cases, however, life might not be so forgiving. It's important to remember that risking our lives or permanently damaging our health in the name of fun is never worth the risk. And this is often the case for kids who—because of boredom or pressure from friends or both—experiment with different ways of getting high. Luckily, most schools and parents make sure that kids understand the dangers of using drugs, which include health damage, brain damage, and death. What is often overlooked, though, are other methods of getting high—methods that don't involve drugs. Some of these methods, as Damian is about to learn, are just as dangerous as drugs, if not more so. The consequences are every bit as severe.

Damian's Story

"Another boring day in a boring town," said Damian as his friend Kyle walked in the front door of Damian's house. Most people didn't understand what it was like to be stuck in the middle of a nowhere town with nothing to do. Kyle understood. That's why Damian liked to hang out with him.

what is often overlooked, though, are other methods of getting high—methods that don't involve drugs.

"I know," Kyle said. "So where are your parents?" Damian explained that his mom had to have an operation recently, and now his dad took her to the doctor every few days to make sure everything was better.

"Oh yeah?" Kyle asked. "Did she bring back any pain pills?"

"Yeah," Damian said.

"Well, let's take some," Kyle said. "If you don't have any pain, then they make you high."

"Whatever. Do you seriously think I'm gonna let you swipe my mom's pain meds? Besides, she'll know if some are missing." Damian wasn't about to gamble on taking something the doctor hadn't given directly to him.

"Okay, well, I know how to get a buzz without any drugs," Kyle said. He explained that all you needed to do was choke someone for a little bit with a belt or a necktie.

"Once you let go, it feels really good. It's called Pass Out," he said. "Wanna try it?"

Think About It

- Is getting high the only solution to boredom? What else could Damian and Kyle do for fun?

- Have you ever heard of a game like Pass Out? What do you know about it?

- Do you think Kyle is a good friend to Damian? Why or why not?

Kyle took off his belt. He wrapped it around his neck and then pulled it tight. His face turned red, then white, then a little blue. His eyes bulged and turned red. Damian was afraid that Kyle might pass out but just before he did, Kyle let go of the belt. "Whoa," he said, spinning around the room. "Cool."

Kyle offered the belt to Damian, but Damian was still a bit unsure.

"Wuss!" Kyle said. Damian wrapped the belt around his neck and pulled. The pressure on his neck felt terrible, and his heart started to race. When he let go, his brain started to tingle, but he thought it felt good. Well, it felt *different*, anyway. He and Kyle started playing Pass Out whenever they felt bored, which turned out to be quite often.

Think About It

- Have you ever done something because you were afraid of being called a wuss? What happened?

- Does Pass Out sound like a healthy or a smart way to pass the time? Why or why not?

One day at school, a man came to speak to Damian's class. He told them a terrible story about how his son died playing something called the Choking Game. What he described sounded exactly like what Damian and Kyle called Pass Out. The man even said the game has many different names. "And even if you don't die, the game damages your brain . . . forever," he told them. "It's worse than a lot of drugs."

Damian was shocked by what the man said. He had no idea what they were doing was so dangerous. But Kyle just laughed. "Don't worry about that guy," he said. "His son was probably a total loser." Kyle told Damian to meet him in the locker room for a quick buzz. Damian wasn't sure. He said he would catch up with him later.

Think About It

- what do you think about how Damian reacted to what the man said about the Choking Game? what do you think of Kyle's reaction?

- Have you ever done something and learned later that it was very dangerous? what happened?

- was Damian right in not going with Kyle to the locker room? what else could Damian have done?

Damian walked up to the table where the man had some pamphlets and other information.

"Do you know anything about the Choking Game?" the man asked him.

"Yeah, I think I heard somebody talking about it once," Damian answered, not wanting to reveal too much.

"Well, don't ever do it, please," the man told him. "And don't let your friends do it either."

"How can I stop other people from doing it?" Damian asked.

Before the man had a chance to answer, one of Damian's classmates burst into the room. "Come quick!" he shouted. "Kyle's in the locker room, and he's not breathing!"

"Come quick!" he shouted. "Kyle's in the locker room, and he's not breathing!"

When they got there, Kyle was slumped on a bench with a belt around his neck while the principal was calling 911.

"Does anybody know how this happened?" the principal asked.

Damian just stood there, not knowing what to say.

Think About It

- How do you think Damian felt when he learned what happened to Kyle?

- Is there something Damian could have done to prevent this? What?

Few people realize how many thousands of families have lost loved ones because of the Choking Game. It's only recently that parents, teachers, and other professionals have become aware of it. And yet, the dangers of the Choking Game are as bad or sometimes worse than even the hardest drugs.

The Choking Game is not a game at all. It is a deadly gamble. When you choke off the blood supply to the brain, you deprive the brain of life. The result is that your brain cells (the stuff your brain needs to work) begin to die. And because these cells don't grow back, the brain damage is permanent. There's no way of telling when you cross the line, so it's easy to go too far. This risk is especially high when people do this alone, though doing it with others is by no means safe.

So if you are doing the Choking Game, stop. If someone you know is doing it, tell him to stop. If he doesn't, then you need to inform someone—a parent, a teacher, or anyone else who can help. You may think it's uncool to rat out a friend, but what you're actually doing is saving a life. And there's nothing cooler than that. Besides, imagine how it would feel to lose a friend because you didn't speak up.

Work It Out

1. Trying the Choking Game even one time can cause permanent brain damage or death. Never agree to go along with it, no matter how much pressure you feel.

2. If you are doing the Choking Game and you can't stop on your own, get help. There are many resources out there to help you get away from this deadly practice.

3. Keep your friends from doing it, too. Under no circumstances should the Choking Game remain a secret. If you know of someone doing it, you need to make sure that he stops, even if it means reporting it to his parents or teacher.

4. Find healthy substitutes. Life is full of activities that will give you joy and will keep you away from dangerous temptations.

The Last Word from MK

When it comes to something like the Choking Game, it's important that you really understand the dangers involved. Hopefully, what you'll take away from this is how important it is to involve yourself with healthy activities and not let so-called friends talk you into something you may or may not live to regret.

7

A New Look

Things have really changed when it comes to clothing and style. These days, there are as many styles for guys as there are for girls. So now you and your peers are under all kinds of pressure to express yourselves through your appearance.

For some, that means conforming to the most popular styles. Others, like Tommy, feel the need to express themselves as individuals. This can mean risking ridicule from others who might not appreciate your creative expression. It's a tougher way to go, and it takes a little more guts to wear clothes that stand out from the crowd, but it's one step toward being comfortable in your own skin. Maybe you don't think about clothes at all, or maybe you can't think about anything else. Either way, as Tommy found out, it is good to look at style as something that makes life a little more interesting.

Tommy's Story

Tommy loved to draw and was really into photography. Recently, he had learned how to use some image editing software by watching his older brother Blake, who was a graphic designer. Tommy loved finding new creative outlets. He saw them as a way to express himself.

But as much as he liked creativity, he never really felt comfortable with the way he dressed. Tommy attended a school where everyone pretty much dressed the same. Lately, his classmates had been following preppy trends and shopping at the same stores at the mall. They wore shirts with logos displayed across the fronts. Tommy halfheartedly wore the same brands. But he never really felt like his clothes reflected who he was, and that disappointed him.

One girl at Tommy's school, Jen, definitely had her own sense of style. Tommy couldn't really explain what was different about her, but

It's a tougher way to go, and it takes a little more guts to wear clothes that stand out from the crowd, but it's one step toward being comfortable in your own skin.

it was obvious that she didn't shop at the same stores as the rest of the kids at their school. Tommy didn't know Jen well, but he respected her confidence to do her own thing.

Think About It

• why do you think Tommy struggles with his clothing choices?

• How important is it in your school to look a certain way? Do you think people make it more important than it should be, or less?

• what do your clothes say about you?

On the first day of the new quarter, Tommy walked into the art studio for his drawing class. As he looked for a place to sit, he saw Jen in the corner. He had never had a real conversation with her before, but he thought now was his chance.

"Hi," Tommy said as he pulled up a stool at the drafting table next to her. "Is it okay if I sit here?"

"Sure," Jen answered, smiling. "Is this your first drawing class?"

"Yeah, but I do a lot of drawing on my own," Tommy replied. "How about you?"

"Same," Jen answered. "I'd like to go to art school someday, so I thought I'd better learn how to draw the right way."

"What do you draw?" Tommy asked.

"Mostly just doodles. But I design clothes, too. My mom taught me to sew, so sometimes I make my own stuff." Jen opened her notebook to show Tommy her drawings. The dress on the page looked exactly like the dress she was wearing.

"Wait, you made your dress?" Tommy asked, impressed.

"Yup," she said, grinning.

Now Tommy knew why Jen always looked different from everyone else. He knew some of the other girls made fun of her for dressing differently, but he thought it was cool she was so sure of herself. Tommy wished he had the guts to dress how he wanted with confidence.

Tommy and Jen talked some more until the teacher started class. They found out they had a lot of similar interests. They sat next to each other every day in drawing class and even started hanging out on the weekends.

Think About It

· why do you think Tommy wanted to sit by Jen? Have you ever found a friend who had a lot of things in common with you?

· why do you think Tommy is glad to meet a girl who is sure of herself?

"Hey, do you want to go shopping?" Jen asked Tommy one day. They were sitting on the grass in Tommy's backyard. Jen was sketching out a new skirt to sew, and Tommy was using his laptop to adjust the exposure on a digital photo.

"Sure," Tommy replied. "I'll ask my mom if she can drop us off at the mall."

"I wasn't talking about the mall," Jen said. "There's a store I want to take you to. We can walk there."

"Okay . . . " Tommy replied, not sure what to think. But he packed up his laptop and went inside to grab his shoes. "Let's go," he said when he came back.

Jen led the way. Soon, they arrived at a thrift store Tommy had passed a hundred times on his way to school. He had never before thought to go in.

Jen swung open the door. "Hey, Pete!" she called to the guy at the front counter. "Got anything new today?"

"Hi, Jen," Pete replied. "Yeah—someone dropped off a whole bunch of hats and shoes. Take a look. They're in the back."

"Thanks!" she exclaimed, pulling Tommy to the back of the store.

Looking around, Tommy saw tons of clothes folded on tables and hanging on racks. None of the clothes looked like things the guys in his class wore, but some of them really caught his eye. Jen took a hat off of a mannequin and put it on Tommy's head. It was flat on top and had a brim that went all the way around—definitely not like the baseball caps all his friends wore.

"Look in the mirror!" Jen urged.

Tommy saw his reflection. He had to admit he looked pretty good.

"It looks awesome!" Jen exclaimed. "None of the guys at our school wear stuff like that."

Exactly, Tommy thought. He would definitely stand out. But he couldn't decide if that was a good thing or a bad thing.

Think About It

- Why do you think Tommy and Jen get along so well?

- Why do you think Tommy is concerned about standing out if he wears a different kind of hat?

- Have you ever worn something that you loved, even if it was a little out of your comfort zone? How did your friends react to it?

Tommy was surprised to find out the hat was only $3. He bought it and wore it home. He was glad Jen had suggested shopping at that store. For the first time in a while, Tommy felt like he was wearing something that reflected who he was.

But on Monday morning, Tommy didn't feel quite so confident. He got dressed and looked at the hat on his dresser. What would the guys say when he walked into homeroom wearing it? Would they like his new look, or would they make fun of him?

Tommy took a deep breath. He grabbed the hat and put it on. *Well,* he thought as he walked out the door, *only one way to find out.*

Think About It

- Why do you think Tommy is so nervous about what his friends will say about his new look?

- Do you ever feel concerned that others will judge you based on what you wear? If so, why?

Tommy was just starting to become aware of fashion and style. So much of how we feel about ourselves is based on what we wear and how we look. Sometimes we are afraid to express ourselves as individuals, so we conform to what everyone else is doing. Finding the look that feels good to you often takes confidence and a willingness to think outside the box, as Tommy found out.

The main thing to keep in mind is that while your clothes and your style might say something about you, it's the person inside that really counts. So while you might give some thought to what kind of person you are and let that guide you in how to dress, you can let yourself have a little fun with changing your look. It's not a matter of life and death, after all. Just keep experimenting. Eventually, like Tommy, you'll get the hang of it.

Work It Out

1. Be comfortable with yourself. Often when we have trouble finding a style, it's actually because we're not sure about who we are. Think about that first and then maybe the type of clothing and style you wear will suggest itself.

2. Approach style with a sense of fun. It's easy to get caught up in how you look, but remember that dressing up is something we're supposed to enjoy. Treat it like a game and you won't feel so much pressure.

3. Don't be afraid to copy. If you're not sure about what you want to wear, it's okay to copy what you see. Eventually, as you get more comfortable, you can branch out into your own individual style.

4. Experimenting is good—don't be afraid to try something new and different. You might even find other people copying *your* look.

The Last Word from MK

I hope Tommy's story has made the idea of fashion and style a little less awkward for you. Dealing with the pressure to dress a certain way can be tough, especially if you want to dress different from those around you. Anyway, it's the person who wears the clothes that's really important. If you keep that in mind, you might find that shopping for a look is actually something you enjoy.

8

The Slim Singer

When most guys think about problems with food, they think about people who eat too much and gain weight. And of course, overeating isn't healthy for our bodies. But some people eat too little, sometimes to the point of starving themselves. This behavior is just as unhealthy as eating too much because, as everybody knows, you can't live without food. People used to think that only girls could have these kinds of eating disorders. But it turns out, as Dinesh can attest, that starving yourself—or *anorexia nervosa*, as it's called—is a struggle that both boys and girls share.

Dinesh's Story

Everyone at Dinesh's school knew he was a great singer. He even sang the national anthem at the conference championship baseball game. But now things were getting serious. He was going to enter the state talent contest.

His parents were talking about reality television shows. Dinesh had high hopes for his future as a singer, and he didn't want to let himself—or his parents—down.

People used to think that only girls could have these kinds of eating disorders.

Dinesh spent a lot of time practicing in front of the mirror. He scrutinized his appearance daily, and he began to think he looked much heavier than most of the singers on television. He began to worry he was too fat to make it as a performer. So he started jogging to school every day and skipping lunch. He weighed himself after every shower to see how much weight he had lost. But it didn't seem like he could lose weight fast enough.

Think About It

- what changed Dinesh's attitude about his body? Do you think Dinesh's new attitude is healthy? why or why not?

- why do you think Dinesh felt so much pressure to succeed? Are there areas in your life where you feel a lot of pressure to win or do well? what are they?

Even though the scale told Dinesh he was dropping pounds, every time he looked in the mirror, he thought he looked bigger. He turned to the Internet to find faster ways to lose weight. Online, he found all kinds of strange advice. Sometimes he would eat only eggs, and for dinner he might eat a burger but leave the bun on his plate. Sometimes he just drank protein shakes. Sometimes he'd tell his mom he ate at a friend's house and that's why he wasn't that hungry. If she pressed him to eat something, he would take his dinner to his room, claiming he needed to study. He'd come back to the kitchen to throw it away when his parents were in the den watching television. A lot of days, he ate nothing at all. He always felt best about himself when he didn't eat—like he had achieved something.

Dinesh started pushing himself even harder in his workouts. He did push-ups and sit-ups in his room at night, telling his parents he was finishing his homework. Dinesh placed a chart over his bed so he could measure his progress.

Think About It

- Why do you think Dinesh lies to his parents about his diet and exercise plans?

- How might it be dangerous to try a diet that is not recommended by a health professional?

- Is working out excessively a problem? How do you know if you are going too hard?

Before long, Dinesh began having trouble at school. Sometimes trying to concentrate made his head hurt. All he could think about was his rumbling stomach. But he would try to forget it and push himself as hard as he could at rehearsals. There were only two weeks left until the talent contest, and he was worried he wasn't prepared enough.

One day after school, Dinesh was rehearsing with Mr. Dulane, the musical director, when he started to feel strange. His head was throbbing, and he felt a little nauseous, too. He ignored it.

"Okay, Dinesh, let's try that last song one more time," coached Mr. Dulane.

Dinesh was exhausted, but he started the song again. When he got to the last note, he threw his fist in the air. Suddenly, everything went black. When he came to, he saw Mr. Dulane and the school nurse leaning over him.

After examining Dinesh, the nurse brought him some water. "What happened, Dinesh?" she asked. "You're much thinner than the last time I saw you. Tell me about what has been going on in your life lately. Have you been sick?"

Dinesh felt weird. He knew something was wrong with his body, so he told the nurse about what he had been doing to lose weight and what he saw when he looked in the mirror. The nurse told him she would call his parents to come to the school for a meeting. Then she asked Dinesh, "Do you know what eating disorders are?" Dinesh was shocked she had even asked him that. He thought eating disorders were something only girls got.

When Dinesh's parents arrived at the school, they all sat down together with the nurse. Dinesh's guidance counselor, Mr. Morris, was there, too.

"I'm concerned about what happened to you, Dinesh," the nurse began. "You've lost a lot of weight recently, and from what you told me about your eating and exercise habits, you haven't been eating enough to keep your body healthy. It's time to make some changes. Consider this a wake-up call."

Dinesh took a deep breath. He was embarrassed, but he confessed that he always felt fat. He wanted to look his best at the state talent contest, but every time he looked in the mirror, he felt like he was gaining weight. Just saying the words out loud made Dinesh realize his habits were not healthy, but he didn't know how he was going to get better because he still wanted to get even thinner than he was. He needed help, and he was thankful his parents, the school nurse, and Mr. Morris were there to get it for him.

Think About It

- Why do you think people associate eating disorders with girls? Why is that dangerous?

- Were you ever unhappy with your weight? What are some healthy things you can do to feel better about your body?

Unhealthy dieting to the point of starving yourself has been linked to a variety of factors. Researchers have found some people are more genetically prone to these kinds of behaviors. The messages they receive from the media, friends, and even parents can bring out those behaviors in them. Sometimes when kids have problems getting the approval of a parent, they can get into some pretty extreme behaviors, such as eating disorders. While people generally associate anorexia with girls, the fact is that about one in ten anorexics is male.

To make matters worse, kids can find a lot of harmful information on the Internet. Some may not know how to separate the good advice from doctors, nutritionists, and other qualified professionals from the bad advice, sometimes given by people who try to encourage dangerous dieting in others! Without help, young people with anorexia face all kinds of dangers: not just loss of concentration, depression, and damage to muscle and bone development, but they can even suffer a heart attack. So if you think you or someone you know might have an eating problem, it's important that you get help right away. It truly is a matter of life and death.

Work It Out

1. Learn what makes a healthful diet. Understand how much a guy needs to eat every day to remain healthy.

2. Learn your ideal weight range. Knowing the range of correct and healthy weights for someone your age and height will help you tell the difference between healthful and unhealthful eating and exercise.

3. Exercise is good, but in moderation. An hour or so of exercise a day is generally considered healthy. If you find yourself exercising too much to the point of injury or to burn off excessive calories, this might be a warning sign.

4. Get help! Eating disorders are too difficult and dangerous to handle alone. If you suspect you have a problem, you need to tell someone about it.

The Last Word from MK

Lucky for Dinesh, he got the help he needed in time. But when it comes to something as important as our health and our lives, we shouldn't rely on luck. Don't ignore the signs of an eating disorder just because you don't think it happens to guys. It does. And the most important thing is getting the right help in time.

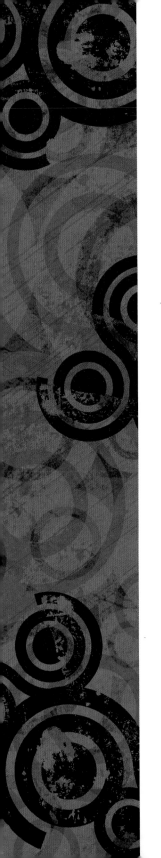

9

The Cupcake Kid

At some point in your life, you'll probably notice that a line gets drawn between activities that are seen as "feminine" and those that are seen as "masculine." Lots of times, if you like to do something that too many girls (and not enough guys) like to do, you might start being ashamed of it. Or, you might even pretend you don't like it because you're afraid of being called a girl . . . or worse.

Figuring out who we are as men isn't easy, especially with all the pressure to act one way or another. But the important thing is not to be afraid or ashamed of who we are and what we like to do. That takes a lot of courage. But, as Mickey learned, there's nothing more manly than that.

Mickey's Story

As Mickey tried to work the lathe in the school's carpentry workshop, he thought about how much he hated the smell of sawdust and the sound of hammering and sanding. Instead, he wished he could be doing something he was good at, such as baking.

Lots of times, if you like to do something that too many girls (and not enough guys) like to do, you might start being ashamed of it. Or, you might even pretend you don't like it because you're afraid of being called a girl . . . or worse.

Mickey had long ago learned how to make peanut butter cookies from scratch. From there, he had moved on to cupcakes, muffins, and even more complicated pastries. Often he would look through his mom's cookbooks for some recipes he could try.

But a few weeks ago, something had happened that made Mickey embarrassed about his love for baking. All the eighth graders were required to take a course in home economics, and they were starting a food unit. Mickey was ecstatic at the thought of learning new baking techniques. But Matt, a guy in Mickey's class, thought otherwise.

"Baking is a total girl thing," Matt said to the guys after class. "Who would want to do something so stupid?"

When Mickey finally signed up for an after-school activity, he did not join the Baker's Dozen, the baking club at his school. Instead, eager to prove that he wasn't into "girly" stuff, he signed up for the Young Carpenters.

Think About It

- Do you think it's okay for Mickey to be interested in baking? Why or why not?

- Are some things automatically girl things and others guy things? What makes it that way?

- Do you think Mickey belongs in the Young Carpenters? Why or why not?

At first, Mr. Slydell, the teacher in charge of the Young Carpenters, tried to give Mickey some extra help. But Mickey didn't seem all that interested in learning about the tools. Finally, Mr. Slydell said, "You know, Mickey, you're more than welcome to be part of the Young Carpenters. But frankly, I'm wondering why you want to. You don't seem to like being here."

"Well, I'm just not sure this is really what I want to do," Mickey answered. "What I really enjoy," he finally admitted, "is baking."

Mr. Slydell laughed. "Well, then what are you doing here?" he asked. "Why aren't you part of the Baker's Dozen?"

"It's all girls in there, and the other guys would think it's weird," he answered.

"Mickey, I can see why you might be embarrassed to sign up for baking club. But just because baking is something that more girls in our school like to do than guys doesn't mean guys can't do it, too. If you like to do it and you're a guy, then that's all you need for it to be a guy thing for you. You might even make it easier for other guys to join."

Mickey had never thought of it that way.

Mr. Slydell told him lots of cooks and pastry chefs were men. "In fact," he added, "I like to whip up a few treats myself on the weekends."

Think About It

- What do you think about Mr. Slydell's advice? Does it make sense to you?

- Have you ever kept something a secret or pretended you didn't like it because you were afraid it was too girly? What was it? What did you end up doing?

With Mr. Slydell's help, Mickey was able to switch clubs. His first project was to make a pineapple upside-down cake. It came out so well that he decided to bring it to the carpentry club and share it. He didn't know if he should admit he made it, but the cake was so popular that it was gone in a few minutes.

"C'mon, Mickey, where'd you get that?" Fong, one of his classmates, badgered him.

"Tell us!" Josh practically shouted. "Did your mom make it?"

"No," Mickey hesitated. "I made it . . . in the school kitchen."

"Seriously?" asked Fong, impressed. "Wow. I wish I knew how to make a cake like this."

"Well, you can learn," Mickey answered. "Why don't you join the Baker's Dozen?"

Think About It

• If some of Mickey's friends thought baking was a girl thing at the beginning of the story, what do you think changed their minds?

• Have you ever changed anybody's attitude about something? What was it? How did you do it?

Like a lot of people his age, Mickey feels pressured to act a certain way. Often, a guy can feel ashamed of doing things that aren't considered manly or masculine. Sometimes other people try to shame us. Other times, because we see these attitudes everywhere, we simply bring this shame onto ourselves. But for Mickey to be able to develop into the man he's meant to be, it's important for him to pursue his interests. Otherwise, his talent would just go to waste.

The funny thing is, there's nothing that really makes any activity—be it baking, knitting, carpentry, or football—manly or girly except for how many boys or girls choose to do it. Sometimes it only takes one or two people to challenge these labels, and suddenly everyone sees that the labels are just silly. Being that first person to stand up can be scary. But if you stay with it, it won't be long until you find other people joining you.

Work It Out

1. Educate yourself. No matter how girly you think your activity is, it's guaranteed that some men and boys have done it before—and probably have done it well. A little research can save you a lot of worry.

2. Share your interest with someone you trust. Having a friend you trust and respect can help you feel better about yourself. Once you share your interest, you often realize it's not so bad. Maybe other guys even share it—or at least admire it—too.

3. Find like-minded people. Look for others who share the same interests you do, whether they are boys or girls. Being around them will make you feel more comfortable.

4. Learn to trust yourself. If you like doing an activity or a hobby, that's more than enough reason to do it, no matter what others might think.

The Last Word from MK

Sometimes we can really drive ourselves crazy trying to figure out what is manly and what is girly, when there really is no such thing. But all we have to do to change that is to be ourselves and be open about it. Strange as it might sound, this might actually be something women know more about than men. That's why today you have female doctors, firefighters, and kickboxers, and nobody thinks too much about it. If they can do it, you can do it, too.

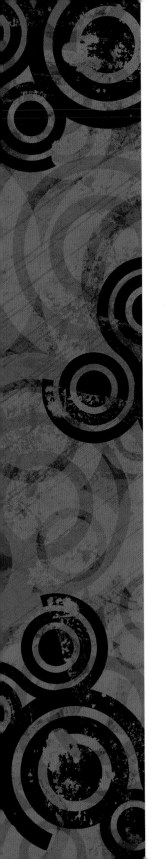

10
The "Short" Stop

When you're young, you get a lot of people telling you what to do: parents, teachers, coaches, camp counselors, maybe even your older brother or sister. So it's natural to think how great things would be if only you were in charge for once, right? Well, not so fast. Leadership comes with its own set of problems. Once you're put in charge of your younger siblings, chosen to organize a party, or made captain of your school team, you suddenly find that out. If you're too friendly, then maybe nobody takes you seriously. And if you're too tough, you might make people afraid of you.

Maybe you feel, as I did, that you're not a natural-born leader. Very few of us are. We might worry whether we have what it takes or how we feel about getting people to follow us. And what about the people you are supposed to lead? They've got their own personality traits, too. The best you can do is take some advice from other successful leaders, and then try to work the rest of it out for yourself. If you can do that, then, like our "short" stop here, you can rise to the challenge.

Max's Story

Max was used to always being the short guy. When it came time for class photos, Max knew he would be put in front. Still, he got good grades, had plenty of friends, and played shortstop on the school baseball team. The other guys would often call him "Shorty," but he knew that was just their way of kidding around. Max was a valuable player to the team. The coach would call him a "thinking player" because he always seemed to position himself just where the batter would hit the ball, and he chose his moments carefully when running or stealing bases.

It was no surprise when the coach announced that he was appointing Max to be team captain. The team cheered. Taylor, the left fielder, patted Max on the head and said, "Way to go, Shorty!" Max threw

Maybe you feel, as I did, that you're not a natural-born leader. Very few of us are.

Taylor's hand off his head and said, "Don't ever call me that again."

"Whoa," Taylor replied. "I'm only trying to congratulate you. Whatever. Chill out, bro."

Think About It

- why do you think Max reacted the way he did? Have you ever treated anyone like that? why?

- why do you think Taylor reacted the way he did? what would you have done?

- was this a happy occasion for Max? why or why not?

Max took his role as captain seriously. If the other guys were supposed to look up to him, Max felt like he needed to step up his game. So when it came time to practice, Max tried to sound really strict, barking commands at his teammates. He felt like he knew how to handle being in charge.

Off the field, though, it was a different story. It wasn't like anybody was being particularly unfriendly, it's just that they didn't seem to come together as much as they used to. One day, Max caught up with Taylor after school and asked him where he was going. "Uh, I'm just going home,"

Taylor said. "I think my mom wants me to help her
with something." Later, Max passed Boss Burgers
and noticed Taylor and his other teammates sitting
around some tables, laughing and eating fries. Max
turned quickly and headed home.

"What happened to you?" his brother Charlie asked him when he got home. "You look like you got hit in the stomach with a line drive." Max was angry with himself for feeling so hurt over what his teammates did. But he was even more embarrassed that his brother could tell right away.

"Can you just shut up?" Max shot back to him as he slammed his bedroom door.

Think About It

- Have you ever found out that people you thought were your friends had all gone somewhere and didn't invite you? What happened? How did you feel?

- Do you think Max is a good captain? Why or why not?

After Max calmed down, he realized he was acting like a jerk. His brother had given him good advice in the past. Charlie had been a team captain and also was the leader of the high school band. Maybe he could tell Max something about being in charge.

"Hey, Charlie," Max said as he hit the couch next to his brother.

"Yeah, what's up?" Charlie responded, looking up from his homework.

"I don't know if I have what it takes to lead my team," Max finally said before the whole story poured out of him. "Everybody always treated me like a little guy, so I thought I should be extra tough now that I'm captain," he told Charlie. "But does that mean I have to give up my friends?"

"Well, it's true that a captain needs to command respect," Charlie said. "But it might also be true that being made captain made you think more about your size than you should. There are many ways to be a big man. Sometimes, that means knowing when to take it easy on people."

Think About It

- Have you ever been treated differently just because of the way you look? What happened?

- What do you think of Charlie's advice? Would you take it? Would you give the same advice to someone else?

The next day, Max saw Taylor standing alone and went over to talk to him. "Hey, Taylor," he said. "I'm sorry I jumped on you last week. I guess I was just worried about not getting respect on the field when I'm trying to lead the team."

"Everyone respects your skills," Taylor said. "It's just that you changed, and nobody is really sure how to treat you . . . or even what to call you!"

Max thought for a minute and said, "Well, as long as you respect me when we're at practice, I suppose you can call me whatever you like. Deal?"

"You got it, Captain Shorty," Taylor said with a grin. "Oh, by the way, the guys are all meeting down at Boss's. Last one there buys!"

Think About It

- Do you think it is good or bad for a team captain to apologize? Does that make Max look stronger or weaker?

- What does respect mean to you? How important is it for a leader to be respected?

Leadership can be very confusing. For most of our lives, we have been used to having one set of people as authorities—our parents, teachers, camp counselors, etc. And another group—our classmates, brothers and sisters, and neighbors—are more or less equals or what we call "peers."

Not only is Max learning to lead, he is also confronting his concerns about his height and how he is viewed by his peers. How does he get people to look up to him when they must always look down? Max is correct to insist on respect, but he has to be careful not to be too harsh. He not only risks his friendships, but it also might be bad for the morale of the team. Finding the right mix is up to every guy to figure out for himself. The important steps Max took were learning to take advice from someone with experience and communicating with his teammates. And humility and good communication skills are important for every leader—no matter what size.

Work It Out

1. Practice good communication skills. Learn to ask questions, speak clearly, and explain yourself in plain language. If people can't understand what you want, you'll never be

able to lead them there. And don't forget to listen, too!

2. Do you know and trust someone who knows how to lead people? Then don't be ashamed to ask for their advice. If not, some schools and other organizations offer leadership training programs where you can learn some basic leadership skills.

3. Don't be afraid to make mistakes, but don't be afraid to correct them either. Apologizing takes courage and humility, but owning up to mistakes is a big part of growing up. Like many things in life, leadership is a lot of trial and error.

4. Set boundaries. Leadership should be respected, but being a leader doesn't automatically make you better than anybody else. Learn to set boundaries for being a leader. Outside of that, just be one of the guys.

The Last Word from MK

Are you ready to take charge? Well, hold on a minute. Leaders must earn respect, not demand it. Start by modeling the behavior you want to see in the people you lead. And remember to leave yourself open to learn from your mistakes. Some of us may be taller, some of us may be shorter, but we can all grow.

I think you can now see that most people seem to struggle with how they want to act versus how they are expected to act (or sometimes just how they *think* they are expected to act!). Hopefully you now have a few more tools to help you find your way.

Certainly, one of the most important of these is communication. Notice how it came up again and again? That's because if you keep things to yourself, it's hard for people to know what you're thinking. It's also hard for you to correct any mistaken impressions you may have about others.

Next, don't be too proud to admit your mistakes and take action to apologize when necessary. Nobody is perfect! Just remember that mistakes can be tools to help us learn how to correct our actions the next time around. So don't live in fear of failure—instead, recognize that mistakes, which are a fact of life, don't have to be regrettable if you choose to learn from them.

Another important tool is the ability to resist peer pressure. Resisting the urge to do something simply because "everybody else is doing it" is one of the most difficult obstacles to overcome when we're growing up. The pressure may take the form of "Guys are supposed to do this," or "Real men don't do that." It takes a lot of inner strength and confidence to keep your head when you hear things like that.

But here's good news: There is a way to totally simplify this problem. First, separate out the activities to avoid because of the obvious dangers to your life and your health. Once you've done that, you are free—as in, free to try, free to succeed, and free to make as many mistakes as you need. Because as long as you're willing to learn from those mistakes, they bring you one step closer to the person you were always meant to be. I wish you well on the journey and hope you remember to enjoy yourself along the way!

Good luck,

MK

Remember, a healthful life is about balance. Now that you know how to walk that path, pay it forward to a friend or even yourself! Remember the Work It Out tips throughout this book, and then take these steps to get healthy and get going.

- Open and honest communication is key. Secrets, lies, and deceit only make problems worse. The first step in resolving any kind of problem is to be open and honest about what the problem is.

- Never be ashamed to admit you don't know something. Nobody is born knowing everything. So when you find yourself confused about something, ask a person you trust about it. You're probably not the only person who doesn't know—it's just that the others were too embarrassed to ask.

- When you need to say no, say it firmly. In some cases, you might feel pressure to do something that's criminal or dangerous, but don't beat around the bush. Look the person in the eye and say no. If the pressure doesn't stop, leave.

- Knowledge is power. The more you know, the better decisions you will make. We are fortunate to live in an information age where so much knowledge is easy to find. But always be careful when getting information from the Internet. Only use trusted and reliable sites.

- Don't be afraid to ask for help. Some serious problems such as drug and alcohol addiction, depression, or anorexia are too difficult for a person to solve on his own. Learn to reach out when you need professional help.

- Accept yourself the way you are. Of course it's fine to want to improve ourselves, whether it's to run faster, learn more, build more muscle, or lose some fat. But never be ashamed of who you are, what you look like, or how you feel.

- Make friends with your mistakes. We can often be very hard on ourselves when we realize that we messed up. Don't be. Mistakes are our best teachers.

- Don't forget that you're a role model, too. While you're looking to others to figure out how to act, others are looking to you. Try to be the best role model you can be and be ready to share what you know with others.

Additional Resources

Selected Bibliography

Adler, Patricia A., and Peter Adler. *Peer Power: Preadolescent Culture and Identity.* New Brunswick, NJ: Rutgers University Press, 1998.

Adolescent Substance Abuse Knowledge Base. 9 July 2010 <http://www.adolescent-substance-abuse.com>.

Further Reading

Erlbach, Arlene. *The Middle School Survival Guide.* New York: Walker & Co., 2003.

Mosatche, Harriet S., and Karen Unger. *Too Old for This, Too Young for That: Your Survival Guide for the Middle-School Years.* Minneapolis, MN: Free Spirit Publishing, 2010.

Teal, Dr. Joyce. *Just Do It Kid.* Pittsburgh, PA: SterlingHouse Publisher, Inc., 2008.

Web Sites

To learn more about navigating social norms and expectations, visit ABDO Publishing Company online at **www.abdopublishing.com**. Web sites about navigating social norms and expectations are featured on our Book Links page. These links are routinely monitored and updated to provide the most current information available.

For More Information

For more information on this subject, contact or visit the following organizations.

Games Adolescents Shouldn't Play (G.A.S.P.)
W321 N7669 Silverspring Lane, Hartland, WI 53029
www.gaspinfo.com
This volunteer organization is dedicated to putting an end to the Choking Game. They provide education, resources, and support.

National Eating Disorders Association (NEDA)
603 Stewart Street, Suite 803, Seattle, WA 98101-1264
206–382–3587
Toll-Free Information & Referral Helpline
1-800-931-2237
www.nationaleatingdisorders.org
Provides education, resources, and support to those affected by eating disorders.

United States Department of Health and Human Services Substance Abuse and Mental Health Services Administration (SAMHSA)
P.O. Box 2345, Rockville, MD 20847–2345
1–877–SAMHSA–7
www.samhsa.gov/shin
Provides information and resources for the prevention and treatment of drug and alcohol abuse.

Glossary

anorexia nervosa
A psychological disorder characterized by unhealthy dieting, especially eating too little.

authority
The power to make or enforce rules; also a person with that power.

brand
A product or goods made by a specific and often well-known company.

budget
A plan for balancing how much money you receive versus how much you are able to spend.

consumers
The way people are referred to in their role as shoppers, either in deciding about what to buy or when they've already purchased something.

depression
An emotional state characterized by sadness, gloom, and lack of energy. Can often require psychological therapy.

eating disorder
A name given to various psychological problems that involve food—either eating too much or too little.

feminine

Referring to behaviors or qualities often associated with women.

logo

A symbol or other mark that identifies a product as having been made by a specific company.

masculine

Referring to behaviors or qualities often associated with men.

moderation

The quality of avoiding extremes.

nutritionist

A professional whose specialty is the relationship of food and diet with health.

peer pressure

The pressure you feel from others around you to do and act as they do; also refers to the act of applying pressure to others to do and act as you do.

Index

About the Author

MK Ehrman is a freelance writer and editor. He has written numerous magazine articles and self-help books for children, teens, and adults.

Photo Credits

Mustafa Hacalaki/iStockphoto, cover, 3; Christy Thompson/Shutterstock Images, 11; Shutterstock Images, 19, 20, 48; Grady Reese/iStockphoto, 27; Gerald Bernard/Shutterstock Images, 29; Monkey Business Images/Shutterstock Images, 33; Hugo Maes/Shutterstock Images, 38; iStockphoto, 41; Joshua Hodge Photography/iStockphoto, 42; Gustaf Brundin/iStockphoto, 51; Aleksandr Stennikov/iStockphoto, 59; Keith Brofsky/Getty Images, 61; Colleen Butler/iStockphoto, 63; Bonnie Jacobs/iStockphoto, 68; Susan Daniels/iStockphoto, 73; Rikard Stadler/iStockphoto, 77; Dave White/iStockphoto, 87; Steve Debenport/iStockphoto, 89; Kristen Johansen/iStockphoto, 95; Matthew Brown/iStockphoto, 97; Morgan Lane Photography/Shutterstock Images, 99